22.95
Gr Valley

D1537458

DISCARD

82674

Central American Immigrants

Hispanic Americans: Major Minority

Central American Immigrants

Frank DePietro

Mason Crest

Mason Crest
370 Reed Road
Broomall, Pennsylvania 19008
www.masoncrest.com

Printed and bound in the United States of America.

First printing
9 8 7 6 5 4 3 2 1

Library of Congress Cataloging-in-Publication Data

DePietro, Frank.
  Central American immigrants / by Frank DePietro.
    p. cm. — (Hispanic Americans: major minority)
  Includes index.
  ISBN 978-1-4222-2317-8 (hardcover) — ISBN 978-1-4222-2315-4 (hardcover series) — ISBN 978-1-4222-9321-8 (ebook)
  1. Central American Americans—Social conditions—Juvenile literature. 2. Immigrants—United States—Social conditions—Juvenile literature. 3. Refugees—United States—Social conditions—Juvenile literature. 4. United States—Ethnic relations—Juvenile literature. 5. Central America—Politics and government—1979—-Juvenile literature. I. Title.
  E184.C34D47 2012
  972.805'3—dc22
                        2011004336

Produced by Harding House Publishing Services, Inc.
www.hardinghousepages.com
Interior design by Micaela Sanna.
Cover design by Torque Advertising + Design.
Printed in USA.

Contents

Introduction

by José E. Limón, Ph.D.

Even before there was a United States, Hispanics were present in what would become this country. Beginning in the sixteenth century, Spanish explorers traversed North America, and their explorations encouraged settlement as early as the sixteenth century in what is now northern New Mexico and Florida, and as late as the mid-eighteenth century in what is now southern Texas and California.

Later, in the nineteenth century, following Spain's gradual withdrawal from the New World, Mexico in particular established its own distinctive presence in what is now the southwestern part of the United States, a presence reinforced in the first half of the twentieth century by substantial immigration from that country. At the close of the nineteenth century, the U.S. war with Spain brought Cuba and Puerto Rico into an interactive relationship with the United States, the latter in a special political and economic affiliation with the United States even as American power influenced the course of almost every other Latin American country.

The books in this series remind us of these historical origins, even as each explores the present reality of different Hispanic groups. Some of these books explore the contemporary social origins—what social scientists call the "push" factors—behind the accelerating Hispanic immigration to America: political instability, economic underdevelopment and crisis, environmental degradation, impoverished or wholly absent educational systems, and other circumstances contribute to many Latin Americans deciding they will be better off in the United States.

And, for the most part, they will be. The vast majority come to work and work very hard, in order to earn better wages than they would back home. They fill significant labor needs in the U.S. economy and contribute to the economy through lower consumer prices and sales taxes.

When they leave their home countries, many immigrants may initially fear that they are leaving behind vital and important aspects of their home cultures: the Spanish language, kinship ties, food, music, folklore, and the arts. But as these books also make clear, culture is a fluid thing, and these native cultures are not only brought to America, they are also replenished in the United States in fascinating and novel ways. These books further suggest to us that Hispanic groups enhance American culture as a whole.

Our country—especially the young, future leaders who will read these books—can only benefit by the fair and full knowledge these authors provide about the socio-historical origins and contemporary cultural manifestations of America's Hispanic heritage.

Introduction

chapter 1
People with a Long History

Lots of different people live in the United States. There are young people. There are old people. There are rich people and not so rich people. There are people who have different religions.

There are people whose families came from Europe. There are people whose families came from Africa. There are people whose families came from almost anywhere you can imagine.

A long time ago, all those different people didn't live in the United States. The United States didn't even used to be called the United States. **Native** people lived on the land. There were different **tribes** all across North America. But then people came from Europe. They took over. Then they made what is now the United States.

Those first people from Europe were immigrants. They came from somewhere else to live in the United States. Since then, many immigrants have come to the United States. There have been Irish immigrants. There have been African immigrants. There have been Polish immigrants. There have been Iraqi immigrants. There have been Mexican immigrants.

The immigrants this book talks about are from Central America. Central America is made up of many countries. There are seven countries in Central America. Each country has its own history. It has its own **culture** too.

Native *refers to the people who lived in North and South America first, before white people came.*

Tribes *are groups made up of many families living together.*

Culture *is the entire system of beliefs, art, religion, and ways of acting that connect a group of people together.*

WHERE IS CENTRAL AMERICA?

It's the narrow strip of land between North and South America. It's below Mexico on a map.

COUNTRIES IN CENTRAL AMERICA

Central America has seven countries. They are Belize, Guatemala, Honduras, El Salvador, Nicaragua, Costa Rica, and Panama.

Really Early History

Central America has a long history. People first came to Central America thousands of years ago. These were the Native people.

At first, these people hunted animals for food. They found vegetables and fruit to pick in the wild. They fished. Many people moved around from place to place. They followed the animals. They didn't build permanent houses because they were moving around all the time.

Later, Native people learned how to farm. Corn was one important plant they grew. There was more food for people to eat now. People had to stay in one place to do all that farming, too. Towns and cities grew bigger because of this.

Big Civilizations

Some groups of people were really successful. They grew a lot of food to feed a lot of people. They had time to do other things. They could build buildings. They could make art. They could write books.

CENTRAL AMERICAN IMMIGRANTS

A street mural in Los Angeles portrays some of the earliest Americans.

Ancient carving of an Olmec king.

These groups of people are called civilizations. A civilization is a large group of people. But not just any group. A civilization has to have things like religion, art, and a government.

The first civilization in Central America was the Olmec. They lived in what is now Mexico and Central America. They built one of the first cities in Central America. They also built pyramids. They look a little like the pyramids in Egypt. The two civilizations built them on their own, though.

The Olmec traded a lot. They wanted things that other people had. They traded for cocoa beans (the main ingredient in chocolate). They also traded for stones called jade and obsidian. Jade is a green stone, and obsidian is shiny black. They used the stones in their art.

Mayan jade.

No one knows what happened to the Olmec. They just disappeared. They could have all died from a disease. Or they could have been attacked. Or they could have just left their cities and moved somewhere else.

Another big civilization in Central America was the Maya. The Maya were actually made up of lots of different groups of people. Each group spoke a slightly different language. But they had a lot in common, too. They all had the same government.

The Maya lived in the northern part of Central America. They were most powerful a little more than a thousand years ago. They ruled over a lot of land and people.

People with a Long History

Ruins of Mayan architecture.

The Maya are most famous for their **architecture**. They built huge cities. The cities had plazas, ballgame courts, and public baths. There were paved roads. The Maya made lakes that held water to water their crops.

The Maya were very smart. They were very interested in calendars and time. They came up with good ways to measure time. Some of their buildings were even built to help them tell time!

Math and writing were important in Mayan culture. The Maya were one of the first civilizations to use zero. They used tree bark as paper to write books. They also wrote on stones.

But the Maya civilization got too big. There were too many people. They needed too much food. The Maya cut down a lot of trees to clear the land for farming. That ruined the environment.

The first encounter between Spain and North America.

People with a Long History 15

Things got bad in general. Cities fell apart. Rulers lost power. But Mayan people didn't all disappear. There are people who live in Central America today who have Mayan ancestors.

A New People

Native people still lived in Central America. They built towns and cities. They grew food. They fell in love and had children. Children grew up. Life went on the way it always had for hundreds of years.

Then, a new group of people arrived. Spanish explorers came to Central America in 1502. These new people would change everything.

Christopher Columbus had just sailed to North America in 1492. He landed in the Caribbean Sea, north of Central America. A few years later he sailed to Central America.

Columbus and his crew met some Natives. They didn't stay around to chat, though! This was Columbus's last voyage. When Columbus left, no one from Europe came to Central America for a while. The Native people must have started to forget about them.

But then, in 1517, the Spanish came back. An explorer named Francisco Hernández de Córdoba sailed to Central America. He brought lots of people with him. These were people who were going to start living in Central America. They were all from Europe.

These new people saw big cities. They saw Native art. They thought the people they saw might be rich. They might have gold or silver. That was what the Spanish wanted.

The Spanish were ready to take over Central America. They wanted gold. They wanted land. They also had lots of weapons. They had guns. They had horses. They had armor.

They had another weapon too, one they didn't even know they had. They had germs! The Spanish brought sicknesses like smallpox with them. Smallpox didn't exist in Central America before the Spanish came. The Natives had never gotten diseases like smallpox. Their bodies couldn't fight the new diseases.

Many Natives died when the Spanish came. They died from diseases like smallpox. They also died fighting the Spanish. The Natives didn't want the Spanish to take their land. They were happy with how things were. Many tribes fought the Spanish. They tried to make the Spanish leave. But the Spanish were too powerful.

The Maya were still around. But not for long. The Spanish conquered them. They destroyed Mayan cities. They tore down artwork. They burned books. They killed people.

Many people died. The Spanish used some of the survivors as slaves. They sent them to other places to work in mines.

It didn't take long for the Spanish to conquer Central America. In just seventy years, the Spanish took over. By the time they were done, almost five million people had died.

The New Central America

After the Spanish came, Central America was different. Spanish people and Native people had children together.

Christopher Columbus.

This young Latin girl has a long and rich heritage.

Their cultures began to mix with each other. Today, Spanish culture is an important part of Central American culture.

Think about all the things the Spanish brought with them. They brought their language. Most people in Central America speak Spanish today. The Spanish brought their religion. Many Central Americans are Catholic, a type of Christianity. The Spanish brought art. They brought **traditions**.

> **Traditions** *are ways of thinking or acting that are handed down from parents to children, and then on to the children's children.*

CENTRAL AMERICAN IMMIGRANTS

Parts of Native life mixed with parts of Spanish life. A whole new way of life was made.

There were other things in the mix too. The Spanish brought Africans with them. They were slaves. African religions also shaped Central American culture. African food did too. So did African languages.

In the new Central America, your skin color mattered a lot. The Spanish thought they were the best because they were white. White people were the most powerful. They had the most money. People with darker skin were seen as less important. People used all sorts of labels for different people. If you had an African mother and a Native father you were called one thing. If you had a Native mother and a Spanish father you were called something else.

There was no such thing as being equal, though! People with darker skin were treated badly. They were poor. People with lighter skin were treated better. They had more opportunities.

Over time, everybody got all mixed together. Today, Central Americans have lots of different ancestors. They have Spanish ancestors. They have Native ancestors. And they have African ancestors.

A Latino mine worker who faced dangerous conditions in his job everyday.

chapter 2
Problems in Central America

The Spanish were in Central America for a long time. Spain was far away, across the ocean. But the Spanish government ruled Central America. It made laws. It made people pay **taxes**. It had a lot to say about how people lived their everyday lives.

People got tired of this after a while. Central Americans didn't want Spain around anymore. They wanted to make their own decisions.

Central Americans went to war. They couldn't just ask the Spanish to leave. They had to fight them. In the end, they won! In 1821, Central America became free. Spain didn't rule the area anymore.

Living with Freedom

Not everything was perfect, though. Spain was gone. But now Central Americans had more problems to solve.

First, they had to make countries. Central America was all one country. It had different areas inside it, called provinces. Each province became a new country.

The new countries tried to work together. That didn't last long. Soon, the countries started fighting each other.

People still weren't equal either. Spain was gone. However, Spanish people were still there. So were Native people and African people. There were still people with lighter skin and people with darker skin.

The people whose families had come from Spain had more money. They owned big houses and farms called plantations. People with darker skin worked on the plantations.

Working on plantations was hard. Workers grew crops like coffee, bananas, and sugarcane (which is what sugar is made from). They worked all day in the sun. They didn't make much money for their hard work.

Plantation owners were rich. They didn't have to work in the fields. That made the workers mad. Over time, they would get so mad that they would fight back. Another problem was the government. Dictators took over many Central American countries. Dictators are people who run the government. They have complete control over the country. Anything they say goes.

Some dictators weren't that bad. But some were very cruel. They used the army to make people scared. They hurt and killed people.

The United States

Central Americans had something else to worry about. They had to worry about the United States. The United States was far away in the north. But it stuck its nose in Central America's business all the time!

lution
1 people
and try to
row their
ment.

Sometimes the United States helped Central Americans. Sometimes it didn't. It could get rid of a dictator. It could give another dictator power. It could send guns to help a **revolution**. It could trade with countries. It could send the United States army to Central America.

Some people liked that the United States was doing things in Central America. Other people didn't like it at all.

Eventually, the United States itself tried to stop being involved in Central America. Presidents Herbert Hoover and Franklin D. Roosevelt started to change what was happening. They stopped sending the army to Central America. They opened up more trade with Central American countries to help them.

CENTRAL AMERICAN IMMIGRANTS

Latina women working in food preparation back in the 1950s.

However, that didn't last long. The United States kept getting involved in Central America. But why? It had to do with money.

The United States cared about things like coffee and bananas. U.S. companies made a lot of money growing coffee and bananas. The United States wanted to make sure companies could keep growing them.

Sometimes dictators helped the U.S. companies keep growing crops. Then the United States helped the dictators.

Sometimes, Central American presidents got in the way of the U.S. companies. Central Americans elected these presidents. They weren't dictators. They were just like the president of the United States. But they were hurting United States companies. So the United States kicked them out.

A customs' card.

CENTRAL AMERICAN IMMIGRANTS

Unfortunately, the United States supported some bad dictators. These dictators helped the United States. In return, the United States helped them. The United States ignored the bad things the dictators did.

Out of Central America

All the countries in Central America were in trouble. There were **civil wars**. There were cruel dictators. Almost everyone was poor. There wasn't enough food. There wasn't enough land to live on. Many people didn't have jobs.

Many South Americans come to the United States for political reasons. They are looking for a safer place to raise their children.

People were scared. They were scared of the dictators who were killing people. They were scared they would starve. Millions of people left their homes. They had to leave, or they would die.

To find somewhere safe, they left their countries. People moved to other nearby countries. Some went to Mexico. Many went to the United States. They had heard there were jobs in the United States. There was supposed to be money. They hoped they could have better lives there.

Civil wars *are when a group within a country fights against the government of that country.*

APPLICATION POR A CERTIFICATE OF IDENTIFICATION

(FORM FOR MALE APPLICANTS)

#152

UNITED STATES OF AMERICA,
THE PEOPLE OF PORTO RICO } ss:
CITY OF NEW YORK

I, _Bernardo Vega_, a NATIVE OF PORTO RICO a
a loyal citizen of the United States of America, hereby apply to the Head of the New Yo
Branch, Bureau of Commerce and Industry of Porto Rico, for a certificate of identification
a citizen of the United States born in Porto Rico.

I solemnly swear that I was born at _Cayey,_
in the Island of Porto Rico, on or about _January 14, 1885_
that my {father/mother} _Antonio Vega_, was be
in _Patillas, P.R._, and is now residing at
Deceased; that I am domiciled in t
United States, my permanent residence being at _286 Ela Belmo_
Ave, Elmont, N.Y.; that I became a citizen of the United Sta
by (1) _Act of Congress of March 2, 1917_
(2)

In case of an accident, _Mrs. Flora Vega_
whose address is _286 Belmont Ave., Elmont, N.Y._, should be notified.

Bernardo Vega
[Applicant's Signature]

Sworn to before me this _2nd_ day
of _November_, 193_6_

M. T. Dardain
Head of the New York Branch, Bureau of Commerce and Industry.

chapter 3
Looking For a Better Life

In today's world, people move all over. Someone born in Russia could move to England. Someone born in India might end up in the United States.

Most people who leave their homes to move to a new country are called immigrants. Immigrants move for a lot of reasons. Some want to find jobs in another country. Some want to move closer to family. Some are looking for an adventure. Some want to go to school.

No matter the reason, immigrants choose to move. No one is telling them they have to move. They aren't in danger if they don't move.

There are other people who move to a new country because they have to. They might be killed if they stay in their own country. It's actually a life or death situation. Maybe there's a war in their country. Maybe there's a dictator. There are lots of reasons.

These people are called refugees. They are not immigrants. The most important thing to remember about refugees is that they have to run away from their countries.

Many refugees end up in the United States. Some of them are from Central America. It isn't hard to understand why people had to run away from there. Dictators took over many Central American countries. They hurt people. They kidnapped them. They killed them. People were scared and moved out of the country.

A lot of them came to the United States. They thought they would be safe there. Maybe they could even find a job and make some money. But it didn't always work out for them.

Denied

If you are fleeing for your life, you're a refugee. But you have to convince other people you're a refugee too. Most important, you have to convince the country where you want to live to let you in.

As a refugee, you get special treatment. Usually, immigrating is a long process. You have to pay money. You have to sign papers. You have to get approved. If you are a refugee you don't have to do any of these things. You can just move. You don't have to fill out paperwork. You don't have to wait a long time.

You even get a little bit of help when you move. It's hard to move to a new country. You don't know the language. You don't know how people live. You

The Migration Department's reception desk back in the 1950s.

don't know what the food is like. Refugees get some help getting used to their new country. Immigrants usually don't.

But it's not always easy to convince the United States that you're a refugee. The United States doesn't always believe that people are really refugees.

The United States didn't believe that a lot of Central Americans were refugees. The United States was actually helping dictatorships in some

CENTRAL AMERICAN IMMIGRANTS

countries. These dictators were killing people. The United States was ignoring that fact.

People from these countries became refugees. They tried to move to the United States. But the United States was pretending that nothing was wrong. It was pretending that the refugees weren't running for their lives. It pretended that they just wanted jobs in the United States. So the United States didn't let them in.

Lots of refugees moved anyway. The United States wouldn't let them in as refugees. But the people didn't have time to immigrate legally. They were afraid they would be killed if they stayed where they were. So they were illegal immigrants. They came into the United States without filling out all the paperwork they were supposed to.

Only a tiny number of Central Americans were let in as refugees. Thousands more came as illegal immigrants.

Immigrating Today

There aren't really dictators in Central America today. People don't have to fear the army coming to take them away. The government won't torture them. It won't kill them.

That doesn't mean there aren't still problems. Many people in Central America are still poor. There are still lots of Central American immigrants. People from Central America want better lives. They still look for better lives in other countries, like the United States.

The big reason that people immigrate is because of money. Lots of people are poor in Central America. They don't have money to go to the doctor. They don't have enough food. They can't get a good education.

Some people think they can make more money in the United States. Sometimes a mother or father moves to the United States. She or he finds a job and sends the money back to the family. It's hard for immigrants to make a lot of money though. Sometimes there's no money to send back.

Back in the 1950s, a customs official examines an immigrant's suitcase.

Crime is also a problem. Thousands of people die because of crime in Central America. That's definitely a good reason to move! Gangs are especially bad. Gangs break into people's houses. They steal cars. They hurt and kill people. It's hard to stop them. Police try, but the gangs are very strong.

People don't want to live in cities or towns with gangs and crime. They want to be safe. They think that moving to another country might be safer than living at home.

Another reason to move is disease. Medical treatment isn't always good in Central America. There is also a lot of AIDS. AIDS is a disease that weakens your **immune system**. People get sick easily with AIDS, and they can die.

*Your **immune system** is the parts of your body that work together to fight germs and keep you healthy.*

This Mexican man lived most of his life in the United States—but was deported for committing a misdemeanor.

People don't want to get AIDS. They don't want their children to get AIDS either. They might get it if they stay where they are. So they decide to move.

Farmers

Lots of people in Central America are farmers. They have little plots of land. They grow enough to feed their families. Maybe they also grow enough to sell some. They sell corn. They sell bananas. They sell cocoa beans.

These farmers make their money by selling what they grow. The farmers sell things to their neighbors. Maybe they take them to a market nearby.

Children living in poverty in Mexico.

A Latino farmworker in the 1950s.

The crowded U. S. border crossing.

There are farmers in the United States too. They sell corn. They sell other vegetables. They sell wheat. All these farmers might make more money if they could sell them to more people. Now there is a law that lets them do that. It is called the Central American Free Trade Agreement. The farmers in Central America can sell to people in the United States. The farmers in the United States can sell things to people in Central America.

It all seems like a good plan. But it doesn't really help Central American farmers. The farmers in the United States can grow things more cheaply. They can grow corn more cheaply for example. Then they can sell the corn for less money.

It costs the Central American farmers more to grow corn. So they have to sell it for more to cover their costs.

If you had a choice between buying the same thing for $2 or $1, which would you pick? Probably the $1. That's what everyone does. People can buy corn for $2 a pound from Central America. Or they can buy it for $1 a pound from the United States. So they buy it from the United States.

CENTRAL AMERICAN IMMIGRANTS

For those living in slums along the U.S. border, America looks like a land of riches.

That means that the Central America farmers don't make any money. They have to stop farming. They have to look for a different job.

People argue a lot about the Central American Free Trade Agreement. It helps some people. It hurts other people. Lots of Central Americans don't like it. They want to fix their countries a different way. Sometimes they move to the United States.

A Hard Life

Imagine living somewhere in Central America. Your parents don't have jobs. You're hungry every day. You're afraid to go outside at night because of gangs. You're sad all the time.

Then you hear about the United States. Someone tells you that life is different in the United States. Everyone is rich. There are lots of jobs. Money grows on trees. Everyone is happy.

So you and your family pack up and leave. You're going to find that better life.

Looking for a Better Life

But your new life in the United States isn't all that great. It's hard to find a place to live. Now you live in a tiny apartment where everything is falling apart. You share a bedroom with your three brothers and sisters. Your dad finds a job in a factory. He works all day, every day. He only makes enough money to pay for the apartment. Your mom works at a fast-food restaurant. She doesn't make much money either. You're still not very happy.

Plus, you miss home. You miss the aunts and uncles and cousins you left behind. Nobody speaks Spanish here. Nobody knows about your favorite places to play in your hometown. Nobody eats the food you love. It's cold here.

This is what happens to many immigrants. They have bad lives where they come from. So they decide to come to the United States. They have a lot of hope. They make the long journey to the United States. Sometimes they find that it's not so great after all.

Marker indicating the border between the U.S. and Mexico.

Legal or Not?

Every immigrant has his or her own story. People come from different countries. They come for different reasons. They take planes, boats, or walk to get here. Some are legal. Others are illegal.

CENTRAL AMERICAN IMMIGRANTS

Police patrol both sides of the Mexican-American border.

What's the difference? Legal immigrants are allowed to be in the United States. They have filled out paperwork. They have family here already. Or they already have a job.

People who apply to be immigrants have to wait. The United States sometimes takes a long time to tell people they can be immigrants. The United States can make them wait for years.

Some immigrants have to leave their homes right away. They don't have any money. They can't wait for ten years. So they decide to immigrate illegally. They don't fill out paperwork. They don't have family in the United States. They don't have a job in the United States already.

It isn't an issue of right or wrong. Illegal immigrants aren't worse people than legal immigrants. It's just that their situations are different.

Lots of immigrants from Central America are illegal. A lot of them walk to get to the United States. It's a long way from Central America to the United States. They have to walk hundreds of miles through Mexico.

Walking is dangerous. Police are waiting to arrest them. It's hot. There's not enough food or water. People get really tired. Gangs attack groups of immigrants, too.

People get caught all the time. If the police catch them, they put them in jail. Or they send them back to their countries. Then they have to start all over.

Some people even die. They have to walk across deserts. They don't have enough water. Or criminals kill them.

It's not all bad news. Not all immigrants walk across the desert. Some take planes. Some take boats. Some take buses. And not all of them end up having a hard time. They find jobs. They get a good education. They get a nice place to live. It's possible, but it's hard.

Hidden Immigrants

How many Central American immigrants are there exactly? We don't really know. In 2000, there were over a million and a half. By now, there are probably a lot more.

It's hard to count all of them. Some of them are illegal. The government doesn't know that they're in the United States. Then it can't count them.

There are also lots more immigrants every day. The number of Central American immigrants shoots up every year. It's hard to keep track of all of them.

Immigrants come from all the Central American countries. The most come from El Salvador.

A stamped passport.

nis/Entré

Visas

Departures

U.S. IMMIGRATION

MAY 17 1993

(CLASS)

ADMITTED

UNTIL

It isn't an issue of right or wrong. Illegal immigrants aren't worse people than legal immigrants. It's just that their situations are different. Lots of immigrants from Central America are illegal. A lot of them walk to get to the United States. It's a long way from Central America

Miami has many Cuban immigrants.

CENTRAL AMERICAN IMMIGRANTS

to the United States. They have to walk hundreds of miles through Mexico.

If something is **stable**, it is steady; things are pretty calm.

Walking is dangerous. Police are waiting to arrest them. It's hot. There's not enough food or water. People get really tired. Gangs attack groups of immigrants, too.

People get caught all the time. If the police catch them, they put them in jail. Or they send them back to their countries. Then they have to start all over.

Some people even die. They have to walk across deserts. They don't have enough water. Or criminals kill them.

It's not all bad news. Not all immigrants walk across the desert. Some take planes. Some take boats. Some take buses. And not all of them end up having a hard time. They find jobs. They get a good education. They get a nice place to live. It's possible, but it's hard.

Hidden Immigrants

How many Central American immigrants are there exactly? We don't really know. In 2000, there were over a million and a half. By now, there are probably a lot more.

It's hard to count all of them. Some of them are illegal. The government doesn't know that they're in the United States. Then it can't count them.

There are also lots more immigrants every day. The number of Central American immigrants shoots up every year. It's hard to keep track of all of them.

Immigrants come from all the Central American countries. The most come from El Salvador.

Salvadorans have several reasons why they want to come to the United States. El Salvador is a crowded country. It has a lot of people who live on not very much land. There's not enough food. There's not enough material to build houses. So many Salvadorans move.

Almost half of Salvadorans are poor. Jobs are hard to find. Sometimes it makes sense to try and get money somewhere else.

Many people from Guatemala also become immigrants. Not very long ago, there was a civil war in Guatemala. People were afraid. They left the country to escape the war.

Now the war is over. But people are still poor. Farmers are especially poor. Some people hope that life in the United States will be easier.

Another country that sends immigrants to the United States is Nicaragua. Many Nicaraguans are running away from violence. There have been violent governments there. There are gangs. There's a lot of crime. It's not safe for some people to live in Nicaragua.

There aren't as many Honduran immigrants. Honduras has been a pretty **stable** country. No dictators. Less poverty. There are still some Hondurans who come to the United States, though.

A student in the United States with an F-1 visa must return to her country when her education is complete.

CENTRAL AMERICAN IMMIGRANTS

Immigrant Communities

It's hard to move away from home. Think about how you'd feel if YOU had to move. Imagine that your family decides to move away from where you grew up. Your parents have to find different jobs. You move to a town where you don't speak the language.

Your new town has different food. Your school is really different. It's hard to get used to everything! You'd probably like it if there was someone else from your town that moved too. Someone who spoke the same language. Someone who knew where you came from.

That's exactly how many Central Americans feel. They miss their homes. They miss their families and friends. When they come to the United States, they try to find other people from home. That's why many Central American immigrants live to-gether in the same city or neighborhood.

Lots of immigrants have done that. There are Italian neighborhoods in a lot of cities. There are Chinese neighborhoods. There are Irish neighborhoods and Polish neighborhoods.

Certain United States cities have more Central Americans than others. There are a lot of Salvadorans in Washington, D.C. Los Angeles is home to Salvadorans and Guatemalans. Lots of Nicaraguans and Hondurans live in Florida and New Orleans.

Education

Education is really important for everybody. It's really important for immigrants too. Immigrants need to learn English. They need to learn about the United States. They need to learn enough to go to college. Then they can get good jobs.

Many Central American immigrants haven't had much education. Maybe they lived out in the country where there weren't any schools. Maybe they had to drop out of school to take care of brothers or sisters.

Some immigrants can't read or write. Most don't have high school diplomas.

Immigrants who are kids have a better chance at a good education. So do the children of immigrants.

Getting a Job

It's hard for Central American immigrants to find good jobs. They usually have to work for not much pay.

If an immigrant is illegal, it's especially hard. They have to work illegally. They can't just apply for a job they find in the want ads. It's illegal to hire illegal immigrants. So most employers don't want to risk it.

Illegal immigrants have to find an employer who wants to hire them. Some places do hire illegal immigrants. They don't have to pay

If a child can learn English, he will be more apt to be accepted by colleges when he is older.

them as much. They don't have to give them things like health care. Hiring illegal workers saves employers money.

But then illegal workers get treated badly. They get bad pay. They can't fight back. If they complain, then someone will find out that they're illegal. Then they'll get sent back to their home country.

Sometimes really educated immigrants come to the United States. They were doctors or lawyers or engineers back in Central America.

Immigrants from Central America *bring* with them the color *and* richness of their *culture.*

45

They went through years of college. But they can't be doctors or lawyers or engineers in the United States.

For example, a woman from Honduras might have been a doctor. She went to medical school She got a certificate saying she can be a doctor. But she didn't get trained in the United States. So her training doesn't count in the United States. She has to go to school all over again.

Most immigrants, even doctors, can't afford to do that. So they end up working at other jobs. They can't do their real jobs. They don't earn much money.

Central American immigrants who came to the United States in the 1950s often ended up working in factories.

CENTRAL AMERICAN IMMIGRANTS

Group of Latino immigrants who recently arrived in the United States back in the 1950s.

Most Central American immigrants work certain jobs. They are construction workers. They are maids. They work in restaurants. They work in factories. Those are the easiest jobs for them to find.

Against the Law

Most immigrants end up being hard workers. They try their best to find jobs. Then they add to society. They build high-rises. They clean houses. They raise families. They go to school.

Sadly, a few end up breaking the law. Just like American citizens, some Central American immigrants do illegal things.

Immigrants are often poor. So some start to steal. Some have had hard lives and make bad choices. Some were criminals before they came to

Looking for a Better Life

the United States. There are lots of reasons immigrants do illegal things.

One big problem is gangs. There are still gangs in Central America. And there are gangs in the United States too. Gangs deal drugs and hurt people. They carry weapons. They scare people.

Gangs are bad because they cause harm. They also hurt immigrants' reputations. Central American immigrants are mostly hard working. They don't deal drugs. They don't carry knives. But a few Central American criminals can make Americans think all immigrants are like that. That's just not true.

Famous Central Americans

Central Americans face some tough things. And lots of them succeed. They do good things in the world. Sometimes they're so successful that they become famous.

There are famous Central Americans who still live in Central America. There are also famous Central Americans who live in the United States.

Politicians

Oscar Arias Sanchez is a famous Central American politician. He is from Costa Rica. In fact, he used to be the president of Costa Rica. He worked on things outside Costa Rica too.

Sanchez grew up in a rich family. But he could still see poverty all around him. He wanted to know why some people were rich and some were poor. He wanted to know why everyone in Costa Rica wasn't equal. He wanted to know why there was so much violence.

He went to college in Costa Rica. Then he went to school in England. He learned all sorts of things in college that would help him.

Then he came back to Costa Rica. He decided to run for president. He promised to give people jobs, houses, and peace. People liked that. So they voted for him. He won.

He was a good president. He tried to help poor people. He was honest. He didn't become a dictator like other presidents. He really wanted peace.

All his hard work paid off. He came up with something called the Arias Peace Plan. Like the name says, this was a plan for peace. Five leaders of Central American countries signed it.

Sanchez won the Nobel Peace Prize in 1987. The Nobel Peace Prize is very important. It is given to someone who has worked for peace.

Sanchez was only president for a few years. Then he became a professor at Harvard University in the United States. He runs the Arias Foundation. The foundation works to make peace around the world.

Another famous politician is Hilda Solis. Solis is an immigrant in the United States. She is part Central American. Her mother is from Nicaragua.

Oscar Arias Sanchez

Solis is a Congresswoman. She works in the House of Representatives. A district in Los Angeles elected her. Her **district** is mostly made up of people from Latin America.

The people she **represents** are mostly poor. Their water is dirty. They can't find houses they can afford. There's a lot of pollution where they live.

A **district** *is an area or section of a city.*

Represents *means that a person stands up for what voters want to happen in the government.*

Hilda Solis speaks as the newly announced U.S. Secretary of Labor.

WHAT DOES LATINO MEAN?

This book talks about Latinos from Central America. A Latino is someone in the United States whose family is from Latin America. Latin America is made up of Mexico. It is made up of Central America. And it is made up of South America. Most Latinos speak Spanish. But not all. People from Brazil speak Portuguese.

There are millions of Latinos in the United States. Some Latinos were born here. In fact, some Latinos' families have lived here since before the United States was born! Other Latinos, though, grew up in another country. Then they moved to the United States as immigrants. Some Latinos were born in the United States, but their parents or their grandparents were immigrants.

Solis has a tough job. She fights to help her district. She wants to clean it up. She wants to find people places to live.

She has come a long way. She was the first person in her family to go to college. After college, she worked in the White House. She helped people understand Latino issues.

Now, she helps other Latino people. She is especially involved in environmental issues. She fights to clean up the environment. She fights for people to pay attention to Latino issues too.

Musicians

Ruben Blades is a musician. He's also a lot of other things.

He started as a lawyer. Then he became a famous musician. Then he went to college and became a politician. Then he became an actor.

Blades was born in Panama. His parents were musicians. He grew up loving music. He knew he wanted to be a musician someday.

His father had different ideas. He wanted his son to be a lawyer. So Blades studied law and became a lawyer. But then he visited the United States. He heard **salsa** music there. He started making salsa music. He became famous for his music.

> **Salsa** is a type of Latino music that has pieces from jazz, rock, and rhythm and blues all mixed up in it.

Blades' songs weren't usually love songs. Instead, he sang about problems. He sang about how people were poor. He sang about the government.

He eventually won two Grammy awards. That's the highest award you can win as a musician.

Later, he went back to school. Then he decided to run for president of Panama. He ran in 1989. He almost won. He came in second.

That ended his political career. He came back to the United States. He returned to singing. He also starred in musicals and movies.

Activists

Central American governments hurt lots of people. Dictators beat up people. They killed them.

Some people fought back. Juan Romagoza is one of them. Romagoza survived being tortured in El Salvador. Then he **sued** his torturers and won!

Romagoza was a doctor in El Salvador. One day he was giving out free doctors' visits. A crowd of people had come to wait. But then the army of El Salvador started firing guns into the crowd for no good reason.

The army arrested Romagoza. They thought he was someone who fought the government. They wanted to lock him up so he couldn't fight anymore.

Then the government **tortured** him. Luckily, they let him go. He was free! But he couldn't stay in El Salvador. The army might find him again.

He moved to California. He didn't have time to apply to be a legal immigrant. He was an illegal immigrant. He had to get to the United States fast.

In the United States, Romagoza started being an activist. An activist is someone who takes action to make things change. They organize protests. They write letters to politicians. They speak out about what they believe.

Romagoza tried to tell the United States government to stop the government in El Salvador. He didn't want more people to be hurt.

A few years later he got a chance to fight the people who had hurt him. He didn't fight them with his fists or guns, though. This time, the fight was in the courtroom. A lawyer got in touch with Romagoza. He told him that he could sue the two men who had hurt him.

...one sued,
...eans he
...court to
...stice.

...one has
...tortured,
...been
...ough
...pain as
...ment.

Flag of El Salvador

The two men had been important in the El Salvadoran government. Then they retired. They came to live in the United States.

Romagoza and two other people sued the men. They told the court how they had been hurt. They won. The court made their enemies give them a lot of money.

Most important, this was the first time a torture **victim** had sued and won. Now, it could happen again. It led to a law that let more victims sue their torturers.

> A **victim** is someone who has been hurt.

chapter 4
The Future

Central Americans face a lot of problems. Immigrants have a lot of tough stuff to face too. But there's good news. Many do find success!

The future for Central Americans and Central American immigrants is hard to predict. It will include more problems. People will still be poor. There will still be violence. Immigrants will still have trouble getting to the United States. They will still have to learn a new language and a new way of life.

There are lots of ways to make Central Americans' lives better. Some people think that making immigration easier is the best way. Central Americans should be able to move away from the problems.

Other people think we should help solve the problems in Central America instead. Someone should end the poverty. Someone should stop the violence. Then people won't want to immigrate. They'll want to stay in Central America.

How do we do this? Who should do it? It's not easy to answer.

Democracy is a benefit of U.S. citizenship.

New American citizens

Changing Relationships

How will immigration change in the future? It's hard to say.

Immigrants will probably still come from Central America. They will still send back money to their families. They will still keep in touch with those families.

Some immigrants might go back to Central America. They didn't really want to leave their homes. They had to because of violence or poverty. They miss home. Now, they have made some money and can take it back with them.

Central Americans want to change their countries. Some immigrants have gone to college. They have new ideas. They go back to Central America. And they start changing things.

Other immigrants like life in the United States. They want to stay here. They work. They raise families. They go to school. They do a lot for American society. They're here to stay.

Time Line

1100 Mayan Civilization is at its strongest in Central America.

1325 Aztecs conquer Mexico.

1438 Inca rule begins in Peru.

1492 Christopher Columbus lands on the island of Hispaniola (Santo Domingo and Haiti).

1503 Hernan Cortes arrives in Hispaniola.

1521 Cortes defeats the Aztecs in Mexico.

1532 Francisco Pizarro conquers the Inca in Peru.

1610 Santa Fe, New Mexico, is built.

1690 First Spanish settlement in Texas is built.

1769 Franciscan missionary Junipero Serra builds the first mission in California. He will eventually build ten missions up and down California.

1817 Simón Bolivar begins his fight for independence from Spain in Colombia, Venezuela, and Ecuador.

1821 Mexico declares independence from Spain.

1845 Texas becomes part of the United States.

1846 Mexican-American War begins. New Mexico (which includes modern-day New Mexico, Arizona, southern Colorado, southern Utah, and southern Utah) becomes part of the United States.

CENTRAL AMERICAN IMMIGRANTS

1868 The Fourteenth Amendment to the U.S. Constitution says that all Hispanics born in the United States are U.S. citizens.

1898 Puerto Rico and Cuba become part of the United States.

1901 Cuba becomes an independent country.

1902 The Reclamation Act is passed, take away land from many Hispanic Americans.

1910 The beginning of the Mexican Revolution sends thousands of Mexicans north to settle in the American Southwest.

1943 U.S. government allows Mexican farmworkers to enter the United States.

1959 Fidel Castro takes over Cuba. Many Cubans immigrate to the United States.

1970s Violence in Central America spurs massive migration to the United States.

1990 President George Bush appoints the first woman and first Hispanic surgeon general of the United States: Antonia C. Novello.

2003 Hispanics are pronounced the nation's largest minority group surpassing African Americans—after new Census figures are released showing the U.S. Hispanic population at 37.1 million as of July 2001.

2006 According to the Census Bureau, the number of Hispanic-owned businesses grew three times faster than the national average for all U.S. businesses.

Find Out More

IN BOOKS

Braman, Arlette. *The Maya: Activities and Crafts from a Mysterious Land.* Hoboken, N.J.: John Wiley & Sons, Inc., 2003.

Foster, Lynn. *A Brief History of Central America.* New York: Facts On File, 2000.

Hamilton, John. *Becoming a Citizen.* Edina, Minn: Checkerboard Books, 2004.

Keedle, Jayne. *Americans from the Caribbean and Central America.* Tarrytown, N.Y.: Marshall Cavendish, 2010.

Shields, Charles J. *Central America: Facts and Figures.* Broomall, Penn.: Mason Crest Publishers, 2008.

Shields, Charles J. *El Salvador (Central America Today).* Broomall, Penn.: Mason Crest Publishers, 2008.

ON THE INTERNET

The Guatemala Human Rights Commission
www.ghrc-usa.org

The Washington Office on Latin America
www.wola.org

The Central American Resource Center (Carecen)
www.carecen-la.org

Centralamerica.com
www.centralamerica.com

Central American Geography
www.ducksters.com/geography/centralamerica.php

National Immigration Law Center
www.nilc.org/nilcinfo

Mayan Kids
www.mayankids.com

Index

Picture Credits

AMAPO: p. 14

Benjamin Stewart: p. 31, 32, 35, 36, 37, 40

Corel: p. 25, 45

The Jesús Colón papers, Centro de Estudios Puertorriqueños, Hunter College, CUNY, photographer unknown: p. 24

The Justo A. Marti Photographic Collection, Centro de Estudios Puertorriqueños, Hunter College, CUNY, photographer unknown: p. 28

John Hill: p. 13

Nightstallion: p. 53

Office of President Barack Obama: p. 50

O.Mustafin: p. 12

PhotoDisc: p. 39, 42, 54, 55, 56

Photos.com: p. 18, 34, 44

The Records of the Offices of the Government of Puerto Rico in the U.S., Centro de Estudios Puertorriqueños, Hunter College, CUNY, photographer unknown: p. 20, 23, 26, 30, 33, 46, 47

Ricardo Stuckert/PR: p. 49

About the Author
and the Consultant

Frank DePietro is an editor and author who lives in upstate New York. He studied anthropology in college, and he continues to be fascinated with the world's cultures, art, and folklore.

Dr. José E. Limón is professor of Mexican-American Studies at the University of Texas at Austin where he has taught for twenty-five years. He has authored over forty articles and three books on Latino cultural studies and history. He lectures widely to academic audiences, civic groups, and K–12 educators.

DATE DUE

			PRINTED IN U.S.A.